Forever Family

by
Kelly & Lindsey Bullard
Illustrated by Brian Bascle

Forever Family

Copyright © 2017 by Kelly and Lindsey Bullard

All Rights Reserved.

Forever Family

by
Kelly & Lindsey Bullard

Illustrated by Brian Bascle

Dedicated to our son, Caleb. You are a constant reminder of God's unending faithfulness!

*Love,
Mommy
& Daddy*

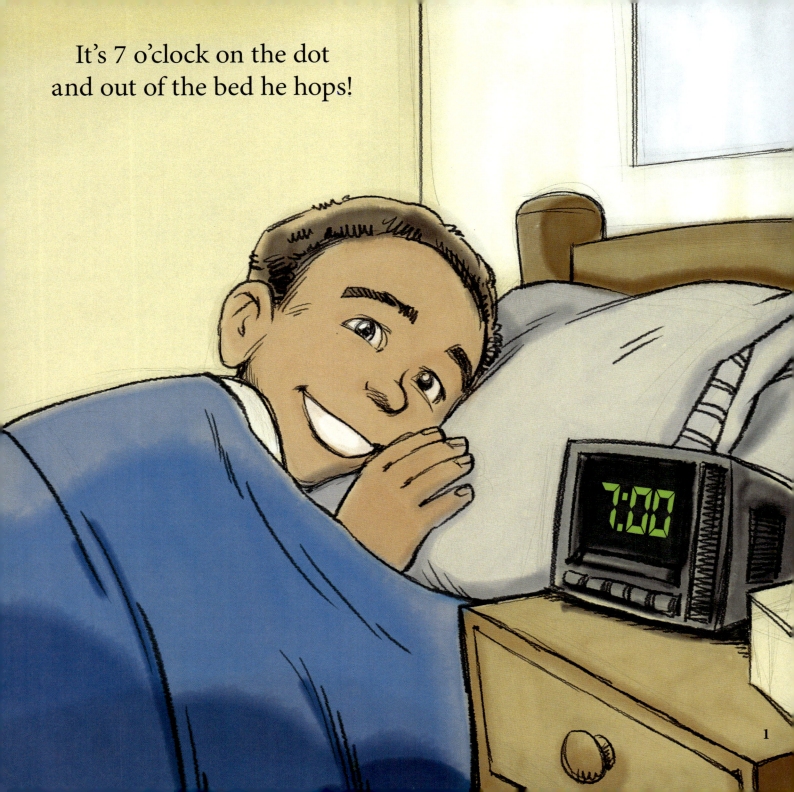

He runs downstairs to mommy and daddy's bed to find a nice warm spot.

But today is not just any day!

It's more special than words can say!

Nope, it's not your birthday
or Christmas Day!

It's even more special,
it's your **Gotcha Day!**

Would your hair be black or blonde?
Would your eyes be brown or blue?

These things and more
went through our mind
as we waited on you!

Then the day came when we got the call that would forever change our lives.

We learned all about you, which made us excited for when you would arrive.

All the painting, decorating, and getting things ready for you, could not compare to the excitement in the air as we waited for your official debut.

Then the day finally came when we would officially meet.

With tears running down and smiles on our faces, we knew our family was complete.

As we held you in our arms, we knew we loved you so.

God placed you in our hearts before we knew you long ago.

With that first look, you had stolen our hearts.

We knew from that moment we would never be apart.

God did something that only God could do.

He brought the perfect child to our family when He gave us you.

Now we are a forever family, not by birth but by love. Just as we are all adopted into God's family to be a part of.

So on this special day,
we thank God above

for sending you our blessing
through His faithful love.

For this child we prayed, and the Lord answered our prayers.
1 SAMUEL 1:27

About the Authors

Kelly and Lindsey Bullard are North Carolina natives. Kelly serves as Senior Pastor of Temple Baptist Church in Fayetteville, NC and holds a Master of Divinity degree from Southeastern Baptist Theological Seminary.

Lindsey is a full-time Independent Sales Representative with Thirty-One Gifts and holds a Master of Accounting degree from the University of North Carolina at Greensboro.

They have one son, Caleb, whom was adopted in 2012.
The Bullards love spending time together traveling and making memories.

To contact the Bullards, please email
bullard.kelly@gmail.com.

Made in United States
North Haven, CT
12 June 2022

20146723R00015